THE VALUE OF DETERMINATION

The Story of Helen Keller

THE VALUE

ILLUSTRATED BY Pileggi

VALUE COMMUNICATIONS, INC.
PUBLISHERS
LA JOLLA, CALIFORNIA

OF DETERMINATION

The Story of
Helen Keller

BY ANN DONEGAN JOHNSON

Second Edition
Manufactured in the United States of America
For information write to: Value Tales, P.O. Box 1012
La Jolla, CA 92038

Library of Congress Cataloging in Publication Data

Johnson, Ann Donegan.
  The value of determination.

  First ed. published in 1975 under title: The ValueTale of
Helen Keller.
  SUMMARY: Focuses on Helen Keller's determination to
hear, see, and speak and her equal determination to help
others with handicaps similar to her own.
  1. Keller, Helen Adams, 1880-1968—Juvenile
literature. 2. Blind-deaf—Juvenile literature. [1. Keller,
Helen Adams, 1880-1968. 2. Blind-deaf.
3. Perseverance (Ethics)] I. Pileggi, Steve. II. Title.
HV1624.K4J63 1976   362.4'092'4 [B] [92]   76-54762
ISBN 0-916392-07-4

Dedicated to Mummy,
whose values I have always admired.

This tale is about an interesting and determined person, Helen Keller. The story that follows is based on events in her life. More historical facts about Helen Keller can be found on page 61.

Once upon a time...

there was a little girl named Helen Keller. When she was a baby, she was bright and lovely, with clear, sparkling eyes, a happy little smile, and a soft baby voice.

Helen's mother and father were very proud of her.
They would watch her and say, "What a beautiful
baby we have!"

Helen grew from a pretty, happy baby into a pretty, happy child. She liked to play with her Teddy Bear. She liked to listen to the tinkling tunes that came from her music box. But then a terrible thing happened.

When she was two, Helen fell sick. She had a terrible fever. Her head ached and was hot. She couldn't eat.

The doctors could not tell why she had that fever. Her worried mother sat by her bed and nursed her, putting cool, wet cloths on her forehead.

At last the dreadful fever left Helen. Mrs. Keller was so happy. Her little girl seemed as well as ever.

But one day when she was bathing Helen, Mrs. Keller noticed a puzzling thing.

"Look, Father," she said. "Helen doesn't close her eyes when I put water on her face. I'm afraid something is wrong. I think we had better take Helen to a doctor right away."

Her mother and father took Helen to the best doctor they could find.

Helen didn't blink when the doctor peered into her eyes. She paid no attention when the doctor rang a bell close to her ears.

"I'm afraid," said the doctor, "that Helen's illness is very unusual. Most sick children soon become completely well. Although it hardly ever happens, the fever has damaged Helen's eyes, and she will never be able to see again."

This was terrible news, but the doctor had not finished. "She is deaf, too," he told Helen's mother and father. "Her ears are damaged, and she will never be able to hear again. It is very unusual and very sad."

There was nothing the poor, sad mother and father could do. They took their beautiful little girl home. When friends came and asked about Helen, the parents told them what has happened.

"Our Helen is blind and deaf," they said. "And because she will never hear, she will probably never learn to talk."

"How awful!" said all their friends. "What will the poor child do if she can't see or hear or talk?"

Helen soon showed what she would do. For her, the world was dark and silent. She felt very much alone and she was very angry.

"I'm going to be a nasty little girl," she said to herself. "In fact, I'm determined. I've made up my mind to do it no matter what happens. I will be a nasty little girl—very nasty." And she threw her toys on the floor and kicked her Teddy Bear.

She wouldn't let her mother wash her face or brush her hair, or even tie her shoelaces.

"Please, Helen!" said her mother.

But of course Helen couldn't hear her, and she went on being dirty and nasty and angry.

"I must get some help," thought her mother.

Helen's mother traveled a long way to a very special school. It was a school for girls and boys who were blind and deaf and mute, just like Helen.

"I have a child who can't hear or see or speak,"
Helen's mother told the man who was in charge of
the school. "What's more, she seems determined to be
as nasty as she can."

"Be glad she has determination," said the man.
"She'll need a lot of it. Children who are deaf and
blind have to try very hard, but they *can* learn to see
and hear in a special way. We have a young lady in
our school who can teach your child to see and hear.
Her name is Ann Sullivan."

Before long, Ann Sullivan came to Helen Keller's home. She wanted to be friends with the angry, wretched child. So she brought Helen a doll.

But Helen roughly snatched the doll out of Ann Sullivan's hands. She was still determined to be nasty, no matter what.

But Ann Sullivan was determined, too. "This isn't going to be an easy job," said Ann Sullivan to herself, "but I *will* teach Helen to see and to hear."

Ann Sullivan let Helen play with the doll for a few minutes. Then Ann took Helen's hand. With her finger she spelled the word "DOLL" on Helen's hand.

"What is she doing?" wondered Helen.

It was the very first time that anyone had tried to teach Helen anything, but she did not understand.

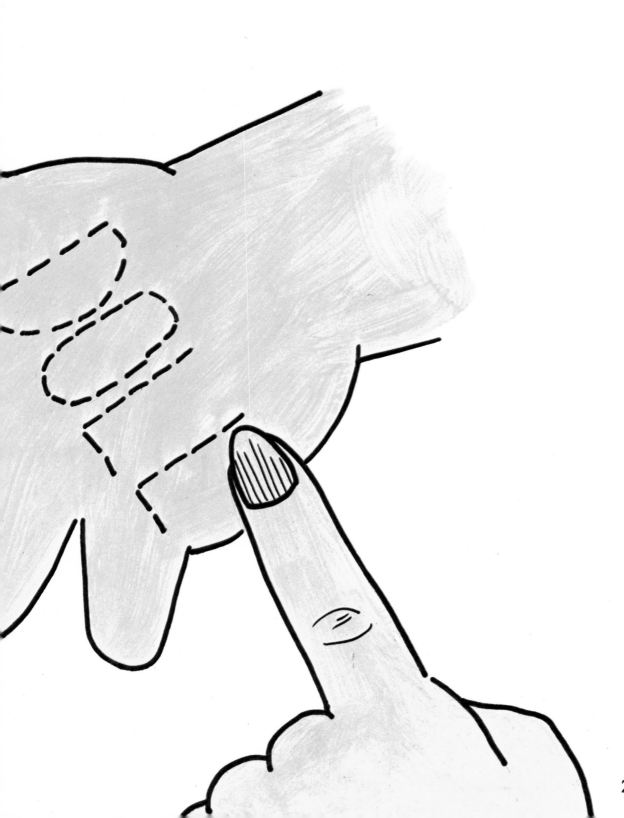

Ann looked at the big house where Helen lived with her parents. She knew that probably everyone in the house pampered and spoiled Helen because she could not see or hear or speak.

"This will not do," said Ann Sullivan firmly. "Helen and I must be alone together while I teach her."

"Very well," said Helen's mother. "We have a little cottage on the grounds. It isn't too near the big house. You and Helen can stay there."

Ann was very pleased, and she took Helen to the cottage. "It will be easier to teach her without any interruptions," she thought. "And I *will* teach her!"

If Ann was pleased with the cottage, Helen was not. Her world was still dark and silent and she was as angry and as nasty as ever she could be.

"I won't let this strange person make me do things I don't want to do," thought Helen. "I'll be so bad that this person will go away. Besides, why should I be good? I don't understand what she's trying to do anyway."

Helen was being especially nasty one day with Ann Sullivan. She was in a terrible rage!

"Oh, dear," thought Ann. "How can I ever make Helen understand that I'm trying to help her."

28

Helen was in such a rage that Ann had to hold her down. Slowly, Helen grew tired. She stopped shouting and fighting. As she lay on her bed, she pretended that she was surrounded by three special friends. She imagined a hearing leprechaun, a seeing leprechaun, and a talking leprechaun.

She sat up, a dirty, rumpled little girl, and for the first time in her silent world, she seemed to hear someone.

"This can't go on forever, Helen," the first leprechaun said.

"You're determined to be bad, but Ann is just as determined to help you learn how to see and hear," said the second leprechaun.

"I wonder," thought Helen, "what determination really means."

"It means not giving up," the third leprechaun said.

Still Helen didn't really understand. But she thought, "Well, being bad didn't work. Perhaps I'll be good for a while and see what happens."

She let Ann Sullivan comb her hair and wash her face. Ann was very pleased. "Helen is trying to be good and to learn new things now," she said to herself. And she kept spelling out words on Helen's hand.

"I hope I am going to understand this soon," thought Helen. "I *will!* I will understand it. I won't give up!"

One day, when Helen was thirsty, she and Ann and the three leprechauns went to the pump for a drink of water.

Ann put a mug into Helen's hand.
She put Helen's hand under the
water that gushed from the pump.
The water flowed over Helen's hand.
It felt good—nice and cool.

Ann took Helen's hand and spelled the word "WATER" on it. Suddenly Helen understood. She had felt the cool water, and then Ann had written on her hand the name of the thing she had felt. Ann was teaching her words.

Helen jumped up and down with joy, and the leprechauns danced in a merry circle. The Hearing Leprechaun was the happiest of the three. He knew that most people hear with their ears, but Helen could now hear in a special way—by having her hand touched.

Helen ran into the cottage she shared with Ann. She touched everything she could reach.

She touched the clock, and Ann wrote the word "CLOCK" on her hand.

She touched a key, and Ann wrote the word "KEY."

She touched the lamp and the chair and everything in the cottage. Ann taught her the words for everything.

The Seeing Leprechaun smiled. "She is hearing with her hand," he said, "and she is seeing with her fingers."

"Nothing can stop you now, Helen," said the Talking Leprechaun. "Someday you'll even learn to speak."

That day had not yet come. First Helen had to learn so many things. She had to learn to spell words into Ann's hand. She had to learn to count. She counted by feeling little beads and pushing them along a wire.

At last it was time for Helen to go to school. Ann went with her, and so did the three little leprechauns. They wanted to remind her to keep trying as hard as she could to be determined—to learn new things and to do what is right no matter what happens.

After Helen had been at the school for a long time, a wonderful thing happened. She learned to speak.

Do you know how she did it?

One of the teachers put Helen's hand to her mouth.

When the teacher said a word, her mouth moved. Helen could feel it move under her hand. Then Helen moved her own mouth the same way.

Then the teacher let Helen's fingers rest lightly on her tongue and her teeth. She said another word, and Helen felt the way her tongue moved against her teeth. While trying to move her own tongue the same way, Helen found she could make sounds. She tried and she tried. And at last Helen said a word.

"She did it! She did it!" cried the Talking Leprechaun. "Helen Keller has learned to talk!"

Helen learned to read, too. Since she could not read with her eyes, as most children do, she read with her fingers. Her books were printed in Braille, with the letters raised up from the page. Helen could feel these with her fingers and know what the letters were.

It had taken all of Helen's determination to learn to hear and to see and to speak, and she knew that there were many other things she had to know.

"When I finish with this school," said Helen, "I will go on to college."

"We'll not go with you, Helen," said one of the leprechauns.

"You don't need us anymore," said another. "We have to go now and help some other little girls and boys."

"I know," said Helen, "but I'll miss you. And I'm so thankful. Because of you, I tried harder when I had trouble understanding."

"Goodbye, Helen," said the leprechauns. "And don't worry. We'll never forget you."

At first Helen was a little lonely for her wonderful leprechauns. But she and Ann Sullivan were very excited about college. Helen was eager to do well, and she did very well indeed. She learned many new things.

Helen never stopped learning —not even after she finished college. She even learned to speak to her friends over the telephone.

One day, at a party, Helen met Mr. Alexander Graham Bell, the man who had invented the telephone. Mr. Bell talked with Helen. She listened, but not in the usual way. She listened by lightly touching his mouth.

And when she spoke, she spoke aloud, as ordinary people do. And she was proud to tell Mr. Bell how she could use the telephone.

Helen and Mr. Bell became good friends. Once, when they were walking in the rain, Mr. Bell asked Helen to put her hands on the trunk of a tree. "Tell me what you feel," he said.

"With the rain falling on the leaves, I seem to feel that the tree moves a little," Helen said. "It makes me think that the leaves are whispering things to one another. It's nice."

Then one day, on a visit to Niagara Falls with Mr. Bell, Helen heard the thunder of falling water in her own special way. She heard it when she felt the ground shake under her feet. Yes, she could even hear with her feet.

Helen was happy. It was wonderful to be able to hear things and see things in her own special way, and to be able to talk about things. She was so glad she had been determined—that she had not given up. She had learned even though learning was very hard for her.

It was wonderful to have Mr. Bell for a friend—and her beloved teacher Ann Sullivan and the little bird named Jonquil that perched on her foot whenever she sat down.

Jonquil was a cockatoo, and it was a gift from Mr. Bell. When it wasn't perched on Helen's foot, it sat on her shoulder and rubbed its head against her face.

Life was pleasant. And yet Helen was not happy. "I have friends," she thought. "I can talk to them. I can tell them what I feel. But I know there are people who can't do this. How I wish I could help them."

Helen Keller *did* help people.

How did she do it?

She did it very simply. She did it by going to people and showing them what she herself had learned.

She wrote books, and she and Ann Sullivan traveled.

When she was in England, she was invited to the palace to meet the King and Queen. "I'd like to be able to read lips," said the King. "Can you teach me?"

"Oh yes," said Helen, and she showed how she could tell what people were saying simply by touching their lips and feeling the way they moved their mouths. It was fun to be able to teach a King and Queen something new.

Even when she was at home, Helen Keller kept working, encouraging others, showing them what could be done.

Once she and her friend Ann Sullivan put on a
vaudeville show. They danced and told jokes.

Helen Keller was especially happy. She knew how *good*
it feels when you have determination.

Helen Keller traveled and spoke to our country's wounded soldiers who had been blinded or hurt during the war. She encouraged them to have determination in their *own* lives.

"You have a problem," she told them, "but everyone in the world has some sort of problem. Those who are determined to work hard can usually cope with their problems. Those who give up—those people who are not determined—are usually very unhappy. Don't let anything discourage you. Keep right on trying. Then you will do what you want to do and you will be happier."

Listening to Helen Keller made other people realize
how hard it must have been for her to learn to "see"
and to "hear" and to "speak" so that others could
understand her.

They said Helen Keller must be a very determined person to do something like that. Just think what it might have been like for Helen if she had not had determination.

Now you may not have to overcome the same difficulties as Helen Keller but just the same perhaps a little determination in your life might bring you happiness, too . . . just as it did for Helen Keller.

The End

HELEN KELLER
1880-1968

Helen Keller overcame the most difficult physical handicaps of being deaf, dumb and blind, and acted as a source of inspiration to those who became aware of her.

When she was born in Alabama in 1880, Helen Keller was a healthy child. She was stricken by a fever at the age of nineteen months and became deaf and blind, and hence mute. She lived in darkness until she was seven. Then her father, who had been a captain in the Civil War and who owned a newspaper, learned that there might be help for Helen.

He and Helen's mother were delighted when that help arrived in the person of Ann Sullivan. Ann could understand Helen's problems, for she herself had been almost blind until, at the age of sixteen, an operation restored her sight. Ann saw that Helen, like many handicapped children, had been greatly spoiled by her parents who felt sorry for her. Ann insisted on discipline for Helen. Later Mrs. Keller was to say to her, "Miss Annie, I thank God every day of my life for sending you to us."

When Helen's father became ill and Helen did not want to ask him for the money for the special schools she needed, one of her admirers came to her rescue and helped raise the funds to send her to school. That admirer was Mark Twain. He was only one of the many people who were inspired by Helen Keller's determination. This quality enabled Helen to learn Braille, to write and even to speak and, in 1904, to graduate with honors from Radcliffe College.

Ann Sullivan, who taught Helen Keller the value of determination, died in 1936 at the age of seventy. After spending almost fifty years with Ann, Helen said of her, "A light has gone out that can never shine for me again."

But Helen now knew the value of determination. She kept working until her death in 1968 to help others. She wrote articles. She gave lectures for the American Foundation for the Blind, and she helped raise a fund of two million dollars for this foundation.

On her eightieth birthday the American Foundation for Overseas Blind honored her. They announced the Helen Keller International Award for those who gave outstanding help to the blind.

A source of personal inspiration to many people, Helen Keller was invited to visit every president who occupied the White House from her childhood on. Her determination, no doubt, was a source of amazement and inspiration even to presidents.

To show how she valued that determination, she once said, "The marvelous richness of human experience would lose something of rewarding joy if there were no limitations to overcome."

The ValueTale Series